GRANDMA GLORIA'S
WOW WOW COOKBOOK

GRANDMA'S DELICIOUS AND EASY SOUTHERN RECIPES THAT WILL WOW YOU

By Gloria Olive

TABLE OF CONTENTS

CASSEROLES

1. Broccoli Casserole

Servings: 8-10 Total Preparation/Cooking Time: 1 Hour 5 Minutes

INGREDIENTS
- 1 large package of broccoli
- 1 can cream of mushroom soup
- 2 eggs
- 2 cups of cheddar cheese, grated
- ½ stick of butter
- 2 cups of cornbread crumbs (Jiffy Cornbread Mix, cooked)
- 2 large chicken breasts
- 2 Cups Water

INSTRUCTIONS
a) Cook broccoli (diced) and chicken (diced) for 20 minutes over low heat. Drain water, set aside, and let cool.
b) Beat eggs, mix in soup, cheese, and eggs.
c) Add the chicken and broccoli.
d) In a saucepan, melt the butter and add the cornbread crumbs.
e) Preheat the oven to 350°F, bake for 35 minutes (covered with foil) uncover and cook for 10 min. This will give the casserole a wonderful crust on top.
f) Enjoy!

2. Gold Hominy Casserole

Servings: 6-8
Total Preparation/Cooking Time: 27 Minutes

INGREDIENTS

- 30-oz can of gold hominy, drained
- 2 tsp of hot sauce
- 1 small can of cream of mushroom soup
- ½ onion, chopped
- 1 small block of garlic cheese
- 1 small package of corn chips

INSTRUCTIONS

a) Put hominy in a casserole dish.

b) Mix soup, cheese, hot sauce, and onion in a pot.

c) Cook for about 6-7 minutes on the stovetop.

d) Pour mixture over hominy.

e) Spread corn chips on top.

f) Preheat the oven to 350°F and bake for 20

g) minutes.
   Enjoy!

3. Corn/Rice Casserole

Servings: 4 Total Preparation/Cooking Time:
40 Minutes

INGREDIENTS

- 1 can of corn
- 1 can cream of chicken soup
- ¾ cup of rice
- 1 cup of grated cheddar cheese

INSTRUCTIONS

a) Prepare the rice according to the package's
   instructions.
b) Combine with the remaining ingredients.
c) Sprinkle grated cheese on top of the casserole.
d) Bake at 350°F for 30 minutes.

4. Lasagna

Servings: 8-10 Total Preparation/Cooking Time: 1 Hour

INGREDIENTS

- 6 cups water
- 2 tbsp salt
- A 1lb box of lasagna (9 noodles), cooked
- 2lb lean ground beef
- ½ cup celery, chopped
- ½ cup green pepper, chopped
- ½ cup onion, chopped
- 2 tbsp oil
- 1 tbsp of dried parsley
- 1 tbsp of dried oregano
- 1 tbsp of dried basil
- 1 teaspoon salt
- 2 tbsp sugar
- 1 tbsp garlic powder
- 1 tbsp black pepper
- 2 eggs, beaten
- 2 cups cottage cheese
- 2 cups grated parmesan cheese
- 2 cups shredded mozzarella cheese
- 2 tbsp tomato paste
- 2 cans diced tomatoes
- 3 cans of tomato sauce

INSTRUCTIONS

a) Preheat oven to 375°F.

b) In a saucepan, brown ground beef. Set aside.

c) In a saucepan, sauté vegetables in oil. Set aside.

d) In a large pot, add tomato paste, diced tomatoes, tomato sauce, salt, sugar, garlic, black pepper, and 1 cup of Parmesan cheese.

e) Add the ground beef and sautéed vegetables, bring to a boil. Simmer on low heat for 8 minutes.

f) In a medium-sized bowl, mix mozzarella cheese, the remaining parmesan cheese, cottage cheese, eggs, parsley, oregano, and basil.

g) Spread a layer of tomato sauce in the bottom of the baking dish, add the next three noodles, then more tomato sauce and cheese mixture before returning to the tomato sauce. (Repeat three times).

h) Cover and bake at 375°F for 40 minutes.

i) Remove from oven, cover the top with mozzarella cheese. Uncover, and bake for 10 more minutes.

j) Enjoy!

5. Meat Lovers Casserole

Servings: 8-10
Total Preparation/Cooking Time: 1 Hour

INGREDIENTS

- 1 cup turkey ham, diced
- ½ cup onion, diced
- 1 cup sausage, diced
- ½ cup red bell pepper, diced
- 1 cup wieners, diced
- ½ cup mixed beans/corn
- 1 can spaghetti sauce
- ½ cup celery, diced
- ¼ orange sauce
- ½ cup broccoli, diced
- 2 tbsp oil
- 1 cup cottage cheese

JIFFY CORNBREAD MIX

- 1 box Jiffy cornbread mix
- 2 eggs
- ½ cup milk
- ¼ cup butter

INSTRUCTIONS

a) In a saucepan, heat 1 tbsp of oil and cook the
b) meats over medium heat for 5-8 minutes. In a separate skillet, add 1 tbsp of oil and cook the vegetables for 3 to 5 minutes over medium heat.
c) Mix the meat thoroughly with all of the sauces.
d) Gently combine the vegetables with the meat and sauce.
e) Place in center of a baking dish, set aside.
f) Combine Jiffy cornbread with milk, eggs, and butter.
g) Coat the baking dish's edges with the cornbread batter.
h) Bake for 35 to 45 minutes at 375°F.
i) Enjoy!

6. Spaghetti Casserole

Servings: 6-8
Total Preparation/Cooking Time: 35 Minutes

INGREDIENTS

- 6 oz spaghetti
- 8-oz can of tomatoes, diced
- 2 tbsp butter
- 6-oz can of tomato paste
- ⅓ cup grated parmesan cheese
- 1 tbsp sugar
- 2 eggs beaten
- 1 tbsp dried oregano, crushed
- 1 cup cotton cheese
- ½ tbsp garlic salt
- 1lb ground beef
- ¾ shredded mozzarella cheese
- ½ cup chopped onion
- ¼ cup chopped green pepper

INSTRUCTIONS

a) Put spaghetti into boiling water with 2 tbsp of salt, cook until tender, drain water and mix in butter, parmesan cheese, and set aside.

b) Cook ground beef, onion and green bell pepper in skillet, drain fat.

c) Add the tomato paste, sugar, oregano, and garlic salt along with the undrained tomatoes.

d) Cook at medium heat.

e) Combine spaghetti, ground beef, and vegetables in a cooking dish, and mix well.

f) Add parmesan cheese and mozzarella cheese.

g) Bake at 375°F for 15 minutes with foil cover.

h) Uncover and bake for 10 more minutes.

i) Enjoy!

SOUPS & STEWS

7. Bean Soup

Servings: 6
Total Preparation/Cooking Time: 1 Hour 15 Minutes

INGREDIENTS

- 1 sm can of butter beans
- 1 sm can of pinto beans
- 1 sm can of kidney beans
- 1 sm can of pork and beans
- ½ lb of ground turkey or ground beef
- ½ lb sausage, your choice
- 1 package of Hillshire sausage
- 1 ½ tbsp mustard
- 2 stalks of celery, chopped
- 1 ½ bell pepper
- 1 large onion
- 2 tbsp of oil

INSTRUCTIONS

a) Combine all the beans in a large pot. Add water to cover 3 in above beans, and cook until soft.
b) In a large skillet, cook all meats and vegetables in oil.
c) Combine meats, vegetables, mustard into large pot.
d) Cover and simmer for one hour over low heat.
e) Enjoy!

NOTE:

If you like beans, you are going to love this soup!

8. Beef Stew

Servings: 6
Total Preparation/Cooking Time: 1 Hour 10 Minutes

INGREDIENTS

- 2 lb lean stew beef meat
- 1 medium bag mix vegetables
- 1 large bell pepper
- ½ onion
- Garlic powder to taste
- Salt and black pepper to taste
- 2 celery stalks, chopped
- 1 large can of tomato sauce
- 2 tsp oil
- 4 medium size potatoes, diced.

INSTRUCTIONS

a) Boil water and add salt, black pepper, onions, celery, and bell pepper.
b) Add the beef and simmer for 45–50 minutes on low heat until it is soft.
c) Add a bag of mixed veggies and cook for 15 minutes.
d) Add the tomato sauce and potatoes.
e) Cook until the soup becomes thick.
f) Enjoy!

9. Chili Beans

Servings: 6
Total Preparation/Cooking Time: 30 Minutes

INGREDIENTS

- 1 cup chopped onion
- 1 brick chili
- 1 cup chopped celery
- 15-oz can of tomato sauce
- 1 cup chopped bell pepper
- 2 tsp sugar
- 2 cups water
- 2 lbs of ground beef
- 3 12-oz cans of pinto beans
- 2 tsp hot sauce

INSTRUCTIONS

a) Sauté onion, celery, and bell pepper in a large saucepan and set aside.
b) Cook ground beef for a few mins and drain fat.
c) Add the sautéed vegetables to ground beef.
d) Add water and brick chili, mix well, and stir constantly.
e) Put the pinto beans, hot sauce, tomato sauce, and sugar in a large pot, and mix.
f) Add all ingredients from the saucepan into the large pot, and mix well.
g) Cook on a stovetop on medium heat for 7-10 minutes. If you like it thick, cook it for 10-15 minutes.
h) Enjoy!

NOTE:

Use any topping of your choice, like cheese, green onions, etc.

SALADS

10. Chicken Salad

Servings: 6
Total Preparation/Cooking Time: 55 Minutes

INGREDIENTS

- 1 ½ chicken breast
- 2 tbsp sweet relish
- 1 small jar of pimento
- 1 tbsp vinegar
- 3 boil eggs
- ½ tsp each of salt and black pepper
- ⅓ cup sandwich spread
- ⅓ cup Miracle whip
- ½ cup chopped onion
- ½ cup chopped celery
- 1 tbsp sugar

INSTRUCTIONS

a) Boil water, add chicken, and cook for 25 to 30 minutes over medium heat, or until the chicken is cooked.
b) Take it out of the water and let it cool before shredding.
c) In a food processor, shred the chicken.
d) Mix all ingredients in a large bowl and stir well.
e) Chill for 15 to 20 minutes before serving.
f) Enjoy!

11. Potato Salad

Servings: 6
Total Preparation/Cooking Time: 20 Minutes

In honor of Mother-in-Law Juanita

INGREDIENTS

- 4 large potatoes, chopped
- 1 small apple, chopped, unpeeled
- 6 boiled eggs, diced
- ¾ cup mayonnaise
- ½ onion, chopped fine
- 1 tsp of mustard
- ½ celery stalk, chopped fine
- 1 tbsp of sugar
- ½ cup sweet radish
- ¼ tsp black pepper
- ½ tsp salt

INSTRUCTIONS

a) Combine all ingredients in a large bowl, mix well, and refrigerate for about 15-20 minutes.
b) Enjoy!

MEATS

12. Homemade Meatballs

Servings: 6
Total Preparation/Cooking Time: 20 Minutes

INGREDIENTS
- 1 lb ground turkey /ground beef
- 2 tbsp flour
- ½ tsp salt
- ¼ tsp Slap Ya Mama or paprika
- ¼ tsp garlic powder
- ¼ tsp parsley flakes
- ¼ tsp oregano

INSTRUCTIONS
a) In a medium bowl, combine all the ingredients.
b) Form small size meatballs in the palm of your hands, rolling 5 - 6 times until formed.
c) 20 to 25 meatballs can be made from 1lb of beef.
d) Heat 1 tbsp of oil in a pan and add 10 to 12 meatballs.
e) Cook the meatballs for 5 to 7 minutes on one side over medium heat.
f) Flip and cook for 3–4 minutes.
g) Place them on a paper-lined plate.
h) Alternatively, you can put the meatballs in a plastic bag and put them in the freezer for later.
i) Enjoy!

13. Barbecue Ribs Three Ways

Servings: 6-8
Total Preparation/Cooking Time: 5 Hours in the Oven, 2 Hours in the Grill

INGREDIENTS

- 4 lbs baby back ribs
- Drizzle of Worcestershire sauce
- Sprinkle of liquid smoke
- 1 tbsp onion powder
- 1 tbsp garlic powder
- 1 tbsp meat tenderizer
- 1 tbsp ground mustard
- 1 tbsp hot paprika l 1 tbsp salt

- ½ tsp salt
- ½ cup brown sugar

INSTRUCTIONS

a) Wash the ribs thoroughly before seasoning.
b) Use a paper towel to dab the surface dry.
c) Liberally sprinkle liquid smoke and Worcestershire sauce over the ribs and thoroughly rub in with your hands.

THE FIRST METHOD(OVEN):

d) Wrap the ribs in plastic wrap four or five times.
e) Place in the cooking dish; do NOT cover.
f) Cook for 4-5 hours at 300°F.
g) Cook it low. Cook it slow.

THE SECOND METHOD(OVEN):

h) Wrap ribs in aluminum foil and cover them with a lid.
i) Cook for 4-5 hours at 300°F.

THIRD METHOD(GRILL):
j) Cook ribs on an outside grill on very low heat.
k) Rotate the ribs every five mins for 50 to 60 mins.
l) Put the ribs in baking dish, wrap them in foil, bake it at 300°F for 45 minutes.
j). Enjoy!

14. Turkey in an Oven Bag

Servings: 6-8
Total Preparation/Cooking Time: 6 Hours

INGREDIENTS

- 1 whole turkey
- 1 tbsp oil
- Table salt, to taste
- Seasoned salt, to taste
- Garlic, to taste
- Basil, to taste
- Black pepper, to taste
- ½ cup onion
- ½ cup celery, diced
- ½ cup green bell pepper, diced

INSTRUCTIONS

a) Rub the turkey thoroughly with oil, front and back.
b) Sprinkle seasoning, to taste, over the turkey.
c) Put onion, celery, and bell pepper in the cavity of the turkey.
d) Place the turkey in an oven bag and put the remaining vegetables on top of the turkey.
e) Bake at 325°F for a 24-lb turkey.
f) Enjoy!

NOTE:

To make your cornbread dressing, use the liquid left in the bag after baking.

COOKING TIME:

l *8-10 lbs: 3 hours*
l *12-18 lbs: 4 ½ hours*
l *20-24 lbs: 6 hours*

SIDES

15. Candy Yams

Servings: 6
Total Preparation/Cooking Time: 1 Hour

INGREDIENTS

- 3-4 medium size sweet potatoes, peeled and sliced
- ¾ stick butter
- 1 ½ cup sugar
- 2 tbsp vanilla extract
- 1 cup water

INSTRUCTIONS

a) Bring water to a boil before adding the potatoes and ensuring they are fully submerged. Do not cover.
b) Boil potatoes for 10-15 minutes and then drain water.
c) Return the pot to the stovetop and mix in remaining ingredients.
d) Cook for 35 to 45 minutes, covered, over medium heat.
e) Enjoy!

NOTE:

The liquid from the potatoes will thicken. Please do not stir at any time.

16. Perfect Cornbread

Servings: 6
Total Preparation/Cooking Time: 30 Minutes

INGREDIENTS

- 1 box Jiffy Cornbread Mix
- ¾ cup milk
- ½ stick butter
- 2 eggs
- 1 ½ tbsp sugar

INSTRUCTIONS

a) Mix all ingredients in a medium-sized bowl, and place in a greased pan.
b) Bake at 375°F for 25-30 minutes.
c) Enjoy.

17. Collard Greens

Servings: 6
Total Preparation/Cooking Time: 1 Hour 30 Minutes

INGREDIENTS

- 4-5 cups water
- 1 ½ tbsp oil
- ½ cup onions, chopped
- ½ celery, chopped
- ½ cup red bell pepper, chopped 2 hot chili peppers. Do not chop 2 tbsp hot chili liquid
- 2 tbsp sugar
- 1 tbsp salt
- 6-8 collard greens' leaves, cut medium size

INSTRUCTIONS

a) Fill a pot with water, bring it to a boil, then turn the heat down to medium.
b) Combine all the ingredients and simmer for 1 1/2 hours or until it's tender.
c) Enjoy.

18. Cornbread Dressing

Servings: 8-10
Total Preparation/Cooking Time: 1 Hour 10 Minutes
In the South, they refer to it as "good old cornbread dressing," and there is nothing quite like it. My mother used the best ingredients, including fresh eggs, fresh milk, fresh vegetables, and homegrown cornmeal. And when she put everything together, the result is wow, wow, wow!

INGREDIENTS

- 1 tbsp black pepper
- 1 medium onion
- 1 tbsp poultry seasoning
- 1 medium bell pepper
- 1 tbsp sage
- 4 sticks of celery, chopped or pureed
- ½ stick butter
- 1 box Jiffy cornbread mix
- 8-10 slices of bread, toasted
- ½ cup flour
- ½ cup cornmeal
- 1 medium can of mushroom soup
- 1 ½ cups milk
- 6 eggs
- 3-4 cups of chicken broth

INSTRUCTIONS

a) In a large saucepan, sauté all vegetables in butter.
b) Add poultry seasoning, sage, and black pepper and cook for 2-4 minutes on medium heat; set aside.
c) In a pot, combine chicken broth and mushroom soup and mix well.
d) In a food processor, blend the cornbread mix, toasted bred, flour, cornmeal and milk or eggs.
e) Mix well with chicken broth and mushroom soup.
f) Put in a covered pan for 40-50 minutes, and bake at 375°F.
g) Uncover and bake for 15 more minutes.
h) Enjoy.

19. Macaroni and Cheese

Servings: 8-10
Total Preparation/Cooking Time: 40 Minutes

INGREDIENTS

- 1 cup heavy whipping cream
- 1 cup half-and-half
- ¼ block grated mozzarella cheese
- ¼ block grated shark cheese
- ¼ block grated mile cheese
- 1 ½ sticks of butter
- 3 tbsp sugar
- ½ tsp Slap Ya' Mama
- 3 tbsp mustard
- ½ tsp garlic
- 1 lb bag of large elbow macaroni

INSTRUCTIONS

a) Bring the water to a boil and season with 1 tablespoon salt. Add the macaroni.
b) Boil macaroni until tender, then drain water and set aside.
c) Add all the remaining ingredients to a large pot.
d) Cook on the stovetop, on medium heat, for a few minutes.
e) Stir constantly until smooth.
f) Pour this cheese mixture over the macaroni and
g) mix well. Put in the cooking dish, spread grated cheese on top, cover, and place in the oven for 25 minutes at 375°F.
h) Remove the cover and bake for 10 more minutes.
i) Cool before serving.
j) Enjoy!

SAUCES

20. Brown Gravy

Servings: 4
Total Preparation/Cooking Time: 20 Minutes

INGREDIENTS

- 6 tbsp oil
- ⅓ cup flour
- ½ cup onions
- 2 tbsp soy sauce
- 2 cups water
- 1 tsp salt
- 1 tsp black pepper
- 2 tsp garlic, chopped
- 3 cups water

INSTRUCTIONS

a) Put the flour and oil in a medium-sized skillet.
b) Cook on medium heat until light brown.
c) Add ½ cup onions and cook for 1 more minute.
d) To brown the gravy faster, add 2 tablespoons of soy sauce.
e) Add water, salt, and black pepper.
f) Cook on medium heat for 10-15 minutes until
g) thick.
   Enjoy.

NOTES

-You can add fried chicken, baked chicken, or pork chops.

-For serving sizes of 6-8, add 2 tablespoons of oil, ½ cup flour, and 3 cups of water.

-If the gravy becomes too thick, you can add more water.

21. Homemade Bar-B-Que Sauce

Servings: 4
Total Preparation/Cooking Time: 10 Minutes

INGREDIENTS

- 1 cup of mustard
- 1 ½ lemon, squeezed
- 1 cup of vinegar
- ½ bottle of Louisiana hot sauce
- 1 cup of Worcestershire sauce l
- 2 tsp of black pepper
- 1 ½ cups of sugar
- 2 tsp of garlic salt
- ¼ cup of oil
- ½ gallon of ketchup

INSTRUCTIONS

a) Combine all ingredients in a large pot.
b) Store in jug/s and refrigerate.
c) Enjoy!

NOTE:
Ketchup should be the last ingredient to be added.

22. Spaghetti Sauce

Servings: 6
Total Preparation/Cooking Time: 7 Minutes

INGREDIENTS

- 1 tbsp oil
- ½ red bell pepper, diced
- ½ green pepper, diced
- ½ onion, diced
- ½ tsp garlic powder
- ½ tsp oregano
- ½ tsp parsley flakes
- 1 tbsp hot sauce
- 1 tbsp sugar
- 12-oz can of tomato sauce
- ½ cup ketchup
- ½ cup water

INSTRUCTIONS

a) In a saucepan, over medium heat, add oil, and sauté bell peppers and onion for 3 minutes.
b) Add garlic, oregano, parsley flakes, and hot sauce.
c) Add tomato sauce, ketchup and water and cook for 3-4 minutes.
d) Enjoy!

DESSERT

23. Apple Pie

Servings: 6
Total Preparation/Cooking Time: 45 Minutes

INGREDIENTS |

- 4 granny smith green apples, sliced small
- 1 tsp vanilla extract
- ½ tsp cinnamon
- 1 tsp lemon extract
- ½ tsp nutmeg
- 1 tsp lemon juice
- 1 tsp cornstarch
- ¾ cup sugar
- ⅓ stick butter
- 2 deep dish pie crusts 9" 12 oz.

INSTRUCTIONS

a) Combine all the ingredients in a large bowl, mix well.
b) Cook the apples on the stovetop, stirring frequently, for 7-8 minutes or until they begin to soften.
c) Arrange the apples from the saucepan into the pie shell.
d) Pour the remaining liquid over the cooked apples.
e) Put the second pie shell on top of the apple-filled pie shell.
f) Pinch around the edges to seal the top and bottom pie crusts.
g) Bake at 375°F for 20-25 minutes or until the crust is brown.
h) Enjoy!

24. Black Berry Cobbler

Servings: 8
Total Preparation/Cooking Time: 40 Minutes

INGREDIENTS

- 2 one-lb bags of frozen blackberries
- 2 cups of sugar
- ½ cup of water
- 1 tbsp of lemon juice
- 1 tsp cinnamon
- 1 tsp nutmeg
- 1 tsp vanilla extract
- 1 tsp lemon extract
- 1 stick of butter
- 2 tbsp cornstarch
- 2 Deep dish pie crusts 9" 12 oz.

INSTRUCTIONS

a) Put all ingredients in a medium pot except cornstarch.
b) Cook for 15 to 20 minutes on medium heat, then add cornstarch.
c) Pour the blackberry mixture from the saucepan into the pie shell.
d) Put the second pie shell on top of the blueberry-filled pie shell and pinch pie shells together.
e) Bake at 400°F for 15-20 minutes.
f) Enjoy!

25. Bread Pudding

Servings: 8
Total Preparation/Cooking Time: 50 Minutes

INGREDIENTS

- 8-10 baked can biscuits
- 6-8 slices of sandwich bread
- 1 ½ cups sugar
- ½ stick butter
- 1 tbsp nutmeg
- 1 tbsp cinnamon
- 1 tbsp vanilla extract
- 1 tsp baking powder
- 1 cup raisins
- 2 eggs, beaten
- 2 cups milk

INSTRUCTIONS

a) In a large bowl, combine all ingredients using a large mixing spoon.
b) Beat eggs and milk well before adding to the bowl.
c) Butter a baking dish and fill it with the mixture.
d) Bake for 30 to 45 minutes at 350°F.
e) Enjoy!

26. Mother's Homemade Ice Cream

Servings: 6

Total Preparation/Cooking Time: 30 Minutes + Chilling Time

INGREDIENTS

- 1 cup sugar
- 3 tbsp flour
- ¼ tsp salt
- 2 ½ cup milk
- 2 eggs
- 2 cups whipping cream

CHOOSE ONE

- 1 ½ tbsp vanilla extract or
- ½ cup chocolate syrup
- ½ cup strawberry syrup

INSTRUCTIONS

a) In a medium size bowl, mix sugar, flour, salt, and milk

b) Cook on medium heat and stir continuously for 20 mins using figure eight stirring.

c) Remove from heat and leave on stove.

d) In a small bowl, beat 2 eggs well. Take 2 tbsp from hot mixture and mix into eggs (repeat this until hot mixture is mixed in fully).

e) Return mixture to stove and cook for 1 ½ minutes then place in refrigerator for 2 ½ hours or overnight.

f) In a large bowl mix whipping cream, sugar and ice cream flavor of your choice.

g) Remove mixture from refrigerator and add ice cream flavor to make custard.

h) Place custard into ice cream maker.

i) Enjoy!

Note: Please refer to video to learn how to set up and use ice cream maker.

27. Mother's Homemade Teacakes

Servings: 8
Total Preparation/Cooking Time: 1 Hour

INGREDIENTS

- 1 ½ sticks of butter
- 1 cup sugar
- 3 eggs
- 2 tsp vanilla extract
- 3 ½ cups flour
- 2 ½ tsp baking powder
- ¼ tsp salt
- ½ tsp Nutmeg

INSTRUCTIONS

a) In a large bowl, beat eggs, vanilla extract, and butter for 3 minutes
b) In a small bowl, combine the sugar, flour, baking powder, salt, and nutmeg.
c) Little by little, mix the dry ingredients into the wet ingredients by hand or using a large spoon.
d) Put the cookie dough in the refrigerator for 35-40 minutes.
e) This process will help the cookies to remain soft after baking. Knead the dough for 2-3 minutes,
f) roll it out, cut it into cookies, and place it on greased cookie sheet.
g) Bake at 375°F for 12-15 minutes
h) Let cool and place in a covered container.
i) Enjoy!

28. Old Fashion Pound Cake

Servings: 12 Total Preparation/Cooking Time: 1 Hour 20 Minutes

INGREDIENTS

- 1 ½ cup cake flour
- 1 cup of milk
- 1 ½ cups all-purpose flour
- 6 eggs
- ½ tsp baking powder
- 1 ½ tsp vanilla extract
- 2 sticks of butter
- 1 ½ tsp lemon extract
- ½ cup Crisco oil
- 3 cups flour

INSTRUCTIONS

a) Combine butter, oil, eggs, sugar, vanilla extract, and lemon extract.
b) Mix flour and baking powder and add to the first mixture.
c) Grease and flour Bundt pan.
d) Bake at 350°F for 1 hour and 15 minutes.
e) Let cool for ½ hour before removing from pan.
f) Enjoy!

29. Peach Cobbler

Servings: 8
Total Preparation/Cooking Time: 1 Hour 5 Minutes

INGREDIENTS
- 3 (29-oz) cans of sliced peaches
- 1 ½ cup sugar
- 1 tbsp cinnamon
- 1 tbsp nutmeg
- 1 tablespoon lemon extract
- 1 tbsp vanilla extract
- 1 tbsp lemon juice
- 1 ½ sticks of butter
- 2 tbsp cornstarch or 2 tbsp flour mixed with 1 tbsp sugar
- 2 boxes pie crust

EQUIPMENT
- 1 pan (13x5.8, 9x3.8)

INSTRUCTIONS
a) Drain the liquid from two peach cans, then put it in a pot with the third can.
b) Add sugar, cinnamon, nutmeg, lemon and vanilla extracts, lemon juice, butter, cornstarch, or flour/sugar mix.
c) Cook on the stovetop for 8- 10 minutes.
d) Put one pie crust in the baking pan.
e) Add the peach filling, followed by the second pie crust on top.
f) Pinch to seal all around the edges using your fingers.
g) Make air holes on the top crust using a fork.
h) Bake at 375°F for 30-40 minutes.
i) Enjoy!

30. Peanut Butter Chocolate Chip Cookies

Servings: 8-10
Total Preparation/Cooking Time: 15 Minutes

INGREDIENTS

- 2 eggs
- ½ cup semi-sweet chocolate chips l
- 1 tbsp vanilla extract
- 2 ½ cups baking powder
- 1 ½ cup sugar
- 3 cups flour
- 1 cup creamy peanut butter
- ½ tsp salt

INSTRUCTIONS

a) In a large bowl, beat eggs, vanilla extract, sugar, butter and peanut butter, set aside.
b) In a small bowl, combine flour, baking powder, salt and chocolate chips.
c) Little by little, spoon in the dry ingredients into the large bowl, mix well using a large mixing spoon.
d) Scoop cookie dough and place onto greased cookie pan 1-2 inches apart.
e) Bake at 350°F for 20-30 minutes.
f) Enjoy!

Note: Use an ice cream scooper to drop cookie dough onto greased cookie pan.

31. Pear Cobbler

Servings: 8
Total Preparation/Cooking Time: 1 Hour

INGREDIENTS

- 3 (29-oz) cans of pears, drained and liquid reserved
- 1 ½ cup pear liquid
- 1 ½ cup sugar
- 1 tsp nutmeg
- 1 tbsp cinnamon
- 1 tsp lemon extract
- 1 tbsp vanilla extract
- 1 tbsp lemon juice
- 1 stick butter
- 2 tbsp cornstarch
- 2 boxes of pie crusts

INSTRUCTIONS

a) Combine all ingredients in a saucepan, except for cornstarch.
b) Cook on the stovetop over medium heat for 7-8 minutes.
c) Remove from stove and add cornstarch. Mix well.
d) Line the pan with one box of pie crust.
e) Put in the pear filling and use the second box of
f) pie crust on top. Use a fork to make an air hole in the top.
g) Bake at 375°F for 35-40 minutes.
h) Enjoy!

32. Ugly Cake

Servings: 10
Total Preparation/Cooking Time: 1 Hour 10 Minutes

INGREDIENTS

- 1 box of Duncan Hines cake
- 4 cups powdered sugar
- 2 sticks butter
- 2 eggs
- 2 boxes of Philadelphia cream cheese
- 2 tbsp lemon juice

INSTRUCTIONS

a) Follow all steps on the back of Duncan's cake box.
b) After mixing, put it in a baking pan and set aside.
c) In a large pan, combine powdered sugar, butter, eggs, cream cheese, and lemon juice. Mix well.
d) Put cheese filling on top of the cake batter.
e) Bake at 350°F for 50 minutes.
f) The best way to store the cake is to refrigerate it.
g) Enjoy!

33. Pumpkin Pound Cake

Servings: 12
Total Preparation/Cooking Time: 1 Hour 15 Minutes

INGREDIENTS

- 1 12-oz can of pumpkin filling
- 3 cups flour
- 2 tsp baking soda
- 1 tsp nutmeg
- 1 tsp cinnamon
- ¼ tsp clove
- ½ tsp salt
- 2 ½ cup sugar
- 1 cup vegetable oil
- 3 eggs

EQUIPMENT

- Bundt pan

INSTRUCTIONS

a) Mix the first 6 ingredients in a small bowl and set aside.
b) In a large bowl, mix sugar with vegetable oil
c) Add 3 eggs (one at a time) and beat well.
d) Add ingredients from the small bowl into the large bowl, little by little.
e) Add 1 can of pumpkin filling, little by little.
f) Bake at 350°F for 50-60 minutes.
g) Allow it to cool for 10 minutes before removing from the pan.
h) This is a wonderful cake with or without icing.
i) Enjoy!

NOTE:
Allow to cool for 30 minutes.

34. Red Velvet Cake

Servings: 12
Total Preparation/Cooking Time: 1 Hour 20 Minutes + Chilling Time

INGREDIENTS CAKE

- 1 ½ cup sugar
- 1 tsp baking soda
- 1 cup of oil
- 1 tsp vanilla extract
- 1 cup buttermilk
- 2 oz of red food coloring
- 2 ½ cup cake flour
- 1 tsp salt
- 1 tsp vinegar
- 3 tsp cocoa

ICING #1

- 1 stick of butter
- 8 tsp Crisco
- 1 cup sugar
- 3 tsp flour
- 2/3 cups milk
- 1 tsp vanilla extract

ICING #2

- 1 stick of butter
- 2 cream cheese
- 2 eggs
- 1 box powdered sugar

INSTRUCTIONS

a) Mix all ingredients by hand. Do not use an electric mixer.
b) Bake at 350°F for 1 hour and 15 minutes.
c) Let it cool for 30 minutes before removing from the pan.

NOTE:
2 cake pans necessary.
Choose one of the two icings.

35. Sweet Potato Pie

Servings: 6 Sweet potato pies
Total Preparation/Cooking Time: 1 Hour 5 Minutes

INGREDIENTS

- 2 medium-sized sweet potatoes
- 1 ¼ cup sugar
- 1 ½ sticks of butter
- 4-5 eggs plus 1 egg
- 1 ½ tbsp vanilla extract
- 1 tbsp lemon extract
- 1 tsp nutmeg
- 1 tsp cinnamon
- 2 deep dish pie crusts

INSTRUCTIONS

a) After cooking, allow sweet potatoes to sit for 10-15 minutes for water to drain.
b) Beat sweet potatoes with beater's blades (wash away strings and repeat 3-4 times).
c) Add sugar, butter, and beat for 1 min.
d) Add eggs, beat for 1 min.
e) Add vanilla extract, lemon extract, nutmeg, and cinnamon and beat well for 3-4 minutes.
f) Transfer batter to 2 deep dish pie crusts.
g) The potato mixture should look like cake batter and taste like ice cream.
h) Bake in a 350°F preheated oven for 55 to 60 minutes.
i) Enjoy!

36. Louisiana Banana Pudding

Servings: 8
Total Preparation/Cooking Time: 25 Minutes

INGREDIENTS

- 1 large box of Jell-O banana pudding
- 3 cups cold milk
- ½ cup Eagle brand condensed milk
- 1 cup Cool Whip
- 8-10 bananas
- 1 ½ box vanilla cookies

EQUIPMENT

- 11 in x 9 in pan

INSTRUCTIONS

a) In a large bowl, whisk the Jell-O pudding and milk.
b) Add condensed milk and whisk well.
c) Add cool whip and whisk.
d) Line the bottom of the pan with cookies, and place sliced bananas on top of the cookies.
e) Put pudding filling on the bananas and repeat this process 2-3 times.
f) Complete with Cool Whip on top.
g) Put in the refrigerator for 15 -20 minutes. This would allow the cookies to get soft.
h) Enjoy!

INDEX

NOTES

Made in United States
Orlando, FL
19 December 2024

56254482R00029